LET'S FIND PULLEYS

by Wiley Blevins

raintree
a Capstone company — publishers for children

MOVE ON UP! WAY UP!

What helped you to move up the hill? A pulley! It's a wheel with a rope wrapped around it. It's a simple machine that moves things.

Pulleys move things up,
down and all around.
Pulleys do work.

WAVE A FLAG

The flag waves high in the air for all to see.

THAT'S WHAT A **PULLEY** CAN DO FOR **YOU** AND **ME.**

LOOK WAY UP!

A crane uses a pulley to lift heavy materials. Cranes help to build great big skyscrapers.

A CRANE TOWERS HIGH IN THE SKY!

NEED TO GET TO THE TOP OF A SKYSCRAPER?

Use a lift! It has lots of pulleys. Press a button.

UP YOU GO!

WHAT DO YOUR EYES SPY?

A window cleaner hangs from a pulley! He moves up and down.

HE SCRUBS UNTIL THE WINDOWS SPARKLE AND SHINE.

PULL. PULL. PULL.

Pulleys can help to build strong muscles. How much can she pull?

IS IT EASY? NO!

PULL ON A CHAIN.

A pulley helps to open
the window shade.
Then up it goes.

LOOK OUTSIDE! WHAT CAN YOU SEE?

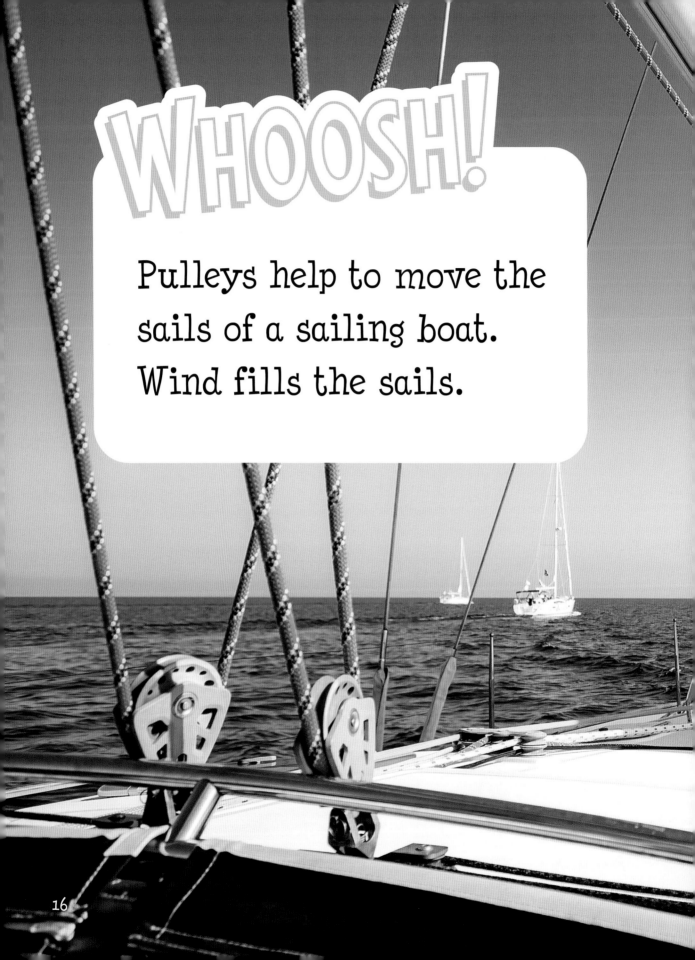

WHOOSH!

Pulleys help to move the sails of a sailing boat. Wind fills the sails.

HAUL UP A BIG CATCH!

Fishermen use pulleys on their boats.

WHAT DID THEY CATCH?

HAVE A GUESS!

DRIP, DRIP, DRIP!

Wet swimming shorts hang in the sun to dry. A clothes line can use a pulley.

TUG THE LINE. MOVE THE CLOTHES ON BY.

**WHEE!**

Go on a zip line above the trees! A pulley makes this ride lots of fun.

CAN YOU FEEL THE COOL BREEZE?

WHAT A THRILL!

You're riding a cable car up a hill. It uses pulleys to move lots of people.

WHAT CAN YOU SPY FROM WAY UP HIGH?

HOP ON THE SKI LIFT!

It's a pulley for people too. Take the lift up the mountain. Hop off and ski back down.

THEN GET
ON THE LIFT
AND DO IT AGAIN!

DON'T LOOK DOWN!

A rock climber needs a pulley. It keeps her safe if she slips.

THAT WAY SHE KNOWS SHE'LL HAVE A GOOD TRIP!

rock climbing pulley

cable car

exercise machine

clothes line

window cleaning pulley

crane

ski lift

sailing boat
pulley

window shade
pulley

flag
pole

zip line

fishing net

lift

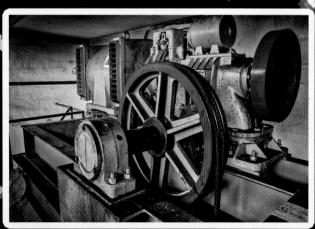

Raintree is an imprint of Capstone Global Library Limited, a company incorporated in England and Wales having its registered office at 264 Banbury Road, Oxford, OX2 7DY – Registered company number: 6695582

www.raintree.co.uk
myorders@raintree.co.uk

ISBN 978 1 3982 0501 7 (hardback)
ISBN 978 1 3982 0502 4 (paperback)

Edited by Erika Shores
Designed by Kyle Grenz
Media Researcher: Tracy Cummins
Production by Spencer Rosio
Originated by Capstone Global Library Ltd
Printed and bound in India

Image Credits
Alamy: Design Pics Inc, 18–19; iStockphoto: BraunS, 30 middle left, DougSchneiderPhoto, 20–21, jonathan_steven, 4–5, Onfokus, 30 middle right; Shutterstock: Africa Studio, 14–15, Andrey Bayda, 16–17, Anetlanda, 31 middle left, Colorshadow, 6–7, ER_09, 22–23, FrameAngel, 10–11, Igor Travkin, 30 bottom right, Jakub Cejpek, 28–29, Laurel A EganssHelen, 31 bottom left, Maxim Petrichuk, 30 top right, MIGUEL MARTINEZ FRIAS, 12–13, momente, 31 bottom right, MrVander, Design Element, RossHelen, 31 middle right, SOLOTU, 31 top right, SvedOliver, 31 top left, TIvanova, 8–9, urosr, 24–25, Various-Everythings, 30 bottom left, Vereshchagin Dmitry, 30 middle, Vixit, 30 top left, Yakubson Petr, Cover, Yana Demenko, 2–3, YanLev, 26–27

British Library Cataloguing in Publication Data
A full catalogue record for this book is available from the British Library.

FIND OUT MORE ABOUT SIMPLE MACHINES BY CHECKING OUT THE WHOLE SERIES!

LET'S FIND INCLINED PLANES

LET'S FIND LEVERS

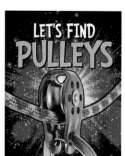
LET'S FIND PULLEYS

LET'S FIND SCREWS

LET'S FIND WEDGES

LET'S FIND WHEELS AND AXLES